# Cowboy Up

## THE POETRY OF THE COWBOY CABARET

by

Steve McAllister

# Contents

# The Wandering Soul – 60

# Blazing The Trail – 72

# Beyond The Horizon – 106

## The Path To Freedom - 126

## The Journey Ahead - 163

# Preface

I started developing *The Cowboy Cabaret* as a one-man performance in which the audience got to select the songs for each show from a deck of custom cards, each with a song I knew how to play. Initially, I improvised the banter I used to introduce each of the songs. However, as I continued to perform the show, I realized I needed something a little more prepared.

I started writing short scripts for each of the songs, and on the fourteenth one, the last line rhymed, reminding me that I was a poet. From there, the rhymes just continued to flow. At the time, I was unaware of the "Cowboy Poetry" movement, but the archetypal character who has returned from beyond the horizon, and my childhood dream of being a cowboy, just seemed to organically fit for the show.

The following poems are mostly based on songs from the show, with a few of the songs I've written over the years thrown in to help balance things out. I've estimated that it would take me over seven hours to perform all of them, but this is the order in which I would if I had a captive audience for that long. I hope you enjoy them and that they inspire you to cowboy up.

Steve McAllister

# THE COWBOY WAY

While the premise for my show started with the idea of the cowboy, it wasn't necessarily just any cowboy. I had grown up with The Lone Ranger, Clint Eastwood, and a number of other cowboy heroes, but it was the overall archetype of the cowboy that has inspired me on how I've lived my life and how these words have come through me.

My concept of the cowboy may be a bit more high-minded and romanticized than most. He is the person who has seen further than others and has had the courage to go beyond where few have gone before. In my mind, the cowboy wasn't just a hired hand who moved cattle from place to place, but the adventurer who explored new routes and sought to improve the world through his experiments in life.

The cowboy lives simply, believing in common sense with a foundation of virtue and honesty. He's not afraid of hard work or hard knocks. Not only does he believe in justice, he has the courage to be its embodiment, protecting the underdogs and standing up for truth.

These days, with so many people following the mainstream ideology of consumerism, it seems as if our highest ideal is stepping in line with the rest of the herd. Personally, I think we need more cowboys. We need to look beyond what has been established in order to blaze trails toward a brighter tomorrow. We need risk takers and people who will not be afraid to do the things that others may say are impossible.

The call to "cowboy up" is for those who see greater potential than what the mainstream has to offer. The cowboy has a vision, and he has the audacity to follow it, regardless of what others may say or think. At a time when society is being guided by people who are as rich in insecurities as they are in material wealth, we need people who are secure in who they are even if they own absolutely nothing but the clothes on their backs.

The songs I've selected are from a variety of influences, but they all touch on the essence of the cowboy in some way. Creedence Clearwater Revival reminds us that the cowboy is not a "Fortunate Son" born into luxury. Willy Wonka follows the vision of "Pure Imagination". Matisyahu prays for peace to come "One Day". And through it all, Blessid Union of Souls says "I Believe" that love is the answer while George Michael invites us to have "Faith."

I believe that what we really need are more people who are willing to "cowboy up".

# Introduction

Before we get too far into this here deal
let me tell you a little bit of my story
I'm one of those fellas that'll risk everything
for a little bit of glory.
I've worn a variety of faces
and seen hands mangle all sorts of time
and I've existed in some way, shape, or form
since man first learned how to rhyme.
I've gone by a number of names,
like Dirty Steve, Wild Will, and Ole Roy.
Y'all can call me anything you want,
but I prefer if you just call me Cowboy.

I'm the spirit of civilization
for better or for worse
and you can blame the spread of nations
on my humble little verse.
I'm the one who heads out alone
to see what's beyond the horizon.
Blazing trails for spreading wealth
is a great way to watch the sun rising.

As a guy whose seen Mother Nature with her bloomers off
and seen plenty more in your cities,
I wanna offer a little perspective
on where you're headed with all your insanities.

Now y'all don't get your dander up.
I speak gospel truth and blatant lies
and if y'all don't yet know the difference yet,
I'm here to help open your eyes.

Before we look to the future
let's talk a bit bout the past
when things were a might bit different
and we had different kinds of pains in our ass.
There were those of us who'd ride the range
out lookin' for adventure.
These days all your ranges are fenced,
and now you wanna wall up the border.

I've ridden through much more simpler times
than all you got going on now,
and how we got from that to this
I'm not quite really sure how.
And though my favorite company
has often been herds of cows
I also know something about humans
and the way we get aroused.

We've always been a pretty emotional bunch,
and we don't always act with reason,
but it's a good thing this world keeps spinning 'round
cuz we can change with every season.

There were times quite long ago
that we all got along a lot better.
We looked out for each other a whole lot more
and felt like we were in it together.
Somewhere along the way,
we added more "us"es and "them"s.
Things got more complicated and separated,
then we started fighting to the death.
One of the problems that most of us have
is that we take ourselves way too serious.
How often we attach ourselves to ideas and to things
tends to make us pretty delirious.
What I'm really hoping you take from these words
is a little break from the life that you know.
I wanna teach you a little about the cowboy way
and maybe even offer some hope.

# Fortunate Son

While I'll be the first to admit
that I am rather entitled,
I'm a white American male from a Christian background
with a million-dollar smile,
but even I don't have it as good
as those who are born to luxury.
Unfortunately, I'm still one of those folks
who's had to put up with my share of drudgery.
It would be nice to live out the high life
and be one of the chosen ones,
but in the game we're playing
only a few of us are born as fortunate sons.

# *Pure Imagination*

The people I've admired most in life
have been those who've known how to dream.
They've been able to see beyond others.
They've created their own plans and schemes.
Cuz when you're making your way in the world,
you've got to be aware of the mainstream.
It's nice that there are people
who want everyone to be on the same team.
But we also need rogues who follow their own path
and manifest their vision
because the most powerful force in humankind
is pure imagination.

# One Day

For a very long time there've been certain people
who've been able to see beyond
the rigmarole that most people endure
that the lust for power has spawned.
As the most insecure among us
have grappled for control
and drawn us into battles
for nations and for souls,
those of us who see further
than the wars that egos enable
and have held onto the vision
of a world that's much more stable,
and though TV makes it hard to see
because they've got to fight for ratings,
the image of war makes money
and gets them masturbating,
we actually are becoming less violent
and have fewer needs for war
except for the greediest few
whom we, for some reason, still adore.

But the vision is expanding
and more people see the way
to make peace in every moment
and make peace with every day.

# I Believe

We've got lots of issues from injustice to poverty
and we ain't found the balance to create true equality.
We're addicted to money and can't get enough of it
and while few of us have it, most of us want it.
While the game may be fixed, we just keep on playin'
but there's a better way of livin', you know what i'm saying.
It ain't about money or keepin' a score.
It's more about givin' so you can have more.
Though unhappy rich folk call down from above,
they don't have the answer.
The answer is love.

# Faith

This life can be full of doubts.
It can also be surprising.
But it shouldn't be a wonder
every morning when the sun is rising
that life is here to provide for us
on our own individual adventures.
You just got to have a little faith in life.
To enjoy the ride, just surrender.

# THE COWBOY IN LOVE

The cowboy believes in love, but he is equal parts romantic and rogue. He has respect for women and loves them honorably, but knows that the divine feminine flows through more than just one of them. While he loves the idea of riding off into the sunset with the love of his life, he's content to ride into the sunset alone and find someone else to love tomorrow. He may not be the best boyfriend or husband material, but he does make the people he loves feel loved.

"Mystery" is the first song I remember writing, as my travel partner Matt Corbin picked out the melody on guitar while we were on our own cowboy journey in Alaska and I mused on the mystery that women offer amid all of life's other mysteries. In offering up the sentiment of how the cowboy feels about women, Michael Jackson sang about "The Way You Make Me Feel", I followed up with the longing ballad "Are You Searching Too?", Marvin Gaye requests to "Let's Get It On", and John Travolta & Olivia Newton-John confirm that "You're The One That I Want".

Eric Clapton reminds the cowboy to tell his love that she is "Wonderful Tonight", Mazzy Star makes us want to "Fade Into You", and Van Morrison invites us to go "Into The Mystic." Luis Fonzi advises us to take love slowly with "Despacito". And while

19

the Monkees ensure us that some women will make us say "I'm a Believer", Elvis Presley tells us how great it feels to be when you're "All Shook Up".

Prince assures our former lovers that we still think about them with "Nothing Compares 2 U", The Temptations humbly offer that they "Ain't Too Proud To Beg," and John Denver asks for one last embrace before "Leaving On A Jet Plane". And, of course, the cowboy praises all kinds of women, as Prince does with the girl in the "Raspberry Beret", John Corbin extols the "Hippie Chick", and Van Morrison reminisces about his "Brown Eyed Girl".

My original song "Happy" celebrates the love of a woman, Smokey Robinson doubles down on a love that lasts with "I Second That Emotion", and Dan Baird tries to simplify things with "I Love You, Period". Little Shop of Horrors reminds us that nice guys have a lot to offer in "Suddenly Seymour".

Unfortunately, love for the cowboy, as with the rest of us, doesn't always go swimmingly. Elvis warns of "Suspicious Minds", Neil Diamond bemoans "Love On The Rocks", Journey gets jealous over "Lovin', Touchin', Squeezin'", and we get into some "real" cowboy music with another Matt Corbin collaboration "Why Did I Chase You Away" and Hank Williams' "I'm So Lonesome I Could Cry". In the end, the cowboy appreciates the idea of true love like "Romeo and Juliet", but stands by the Dire Straights version and stays open to other opportunities.

# Mystery

I've seen a lot of things in the world that have boggled my mind,
everything from the edges of space
to the true constraints of time.
But nothing I have seen
has brought me such damn consternation
as what it is that makes women tick
and draw so much adoration.
They're the fairer of our species
and we've kept them from having control
over everything we do and say and how often we roll.
I'm not quite sure how we've made it this far
keepin' them from makin' decisions,
but it probably has something to do
with why we're goin' broke and runnin' out of provisions.
Though I may never understand
what the mystery's all about,
I feel that my time is the most well spent
when I'm tryin' to figure it out.

Angels and devils and boxes of sand
blankets of snow and the Marathon Man
white hooded klansmen on a cold southern night
these are a few of the mysteries of life.
There's good and there's evil
indifferent are some
mile-high waters and a red midnight sun
upside-down kingdoms and a homecoming queen
these are a few of the mysteries I've seen.

The French Foreign Legion and mother of pearl
three lovely daughters, the youngest in curls
The National Enquirer just covers the flaws
these are a few of the mysteries I saw.
There's a boy and a gun and a red traffic light
miles of pavement, no parking in sight
a lovely young lady just gives it away
these are a few of the mysteries today.

Does strawberry gold dust cover your head?
Do you think of me when you lie in your bed?
Do you embrace the morning with your lips wet with dew?
This is just part of the mystery of you

So many things come into my view
none of them so enigmatic as you.

I see the world
through rose-colored glasses
you see the world as shiny and new.
What could you see
in a poor, country minstrel?
This is just part of the mystery of you.

# The Way You Make Me Feel

There's something about a woman that makes me feel so good.
Though I do complain about 'em,
I'm glad they're here so knock on wood.
While I haven't quite yet figured out
why they need so many shoes,
how they can make me sing for joy and have to sing the blues,
they are quite the conundrum, this other sex so fair
I don't even mind the ones that don't shave their leg hair.
While there are some that are prettier than others
and some that ain't quite cute,
women got it goin' on, and they even got boobs to boot.
While I like hangin' out with the fellas,
and those friendships are real,
I'd much rather spend time with women
for the way they make me feel.

# Are You Searching Too?

There's a fantasy we're told as children
through all of our fairy tales
that true love is waiting for each of us.
It's the wind that fills our sails.

So we spend our lives in constant search
as we try to find the one
as if they can complete us
and our purpose will be done.

And though I think it's idealistic
to put so much stock in just one person,
that they're the key to make us who we are
to make us the perfect version
of ourselves or who we're supposed to be
so that we can feel complete,
the idea does sound rather tempting

I'd really love to meet
someone who can be all of those things
someone who'll be my true blue
so though it's probably a long shot
I'm wondering,
are you searching too?

All that I can give you is my time
and all my heart and soul
and everything I am
sometimes it ain't much,
I think I've lost enough
can you tell me what's in store
if I give it away once more
or are you searchin' too?

Can you make my wandering end?
Are you here as a friend?
Are you another foe, another closing door
another stop along the way, the end to another day
a day I'll come to rue, or are you searching too?

Can I stop this infernal search?
Are your stained eyes my church?
Are you a goddess I can praise, a love to last my days?
Is sanctuary in your arms and comfort in your smile
or should I walk another mile to find what my heart needs,
a way to make me bleed, are you the answer to my call
are you my all in all, or are you searching too?

What's a broken man to do, could I say I love you?
I've been alone so long, my rights have all been wrong.
Will you listen to my song or will you hum another tune?
Oh, have you sung the blues, are you searching too?

Do I find cause to celebrate, is it too soon to wait
for an answer to my plea of who you are to me
or should I be more concerned with the lessons that i've learned
the times that I've been hurt and old flames that have burned
or should I try to see instead of what you are to me
what I can be for you, are you searching too?

Do the scars upon your heart rip when it beats?
Have you been fooled by cheats?
Have you been hurt before, are you afraid of more?
Cuz what I'm lookin' for is time tested and true
and I'm looking right at you, are you searching too?

# Let's Get It On

There's a lot to be said for eye contact
and the messages it can convey,
and some are quite skilled to use body language
to express what they have to say,
but some of us can be rather dimwitted
because our attention span is gone
so sometimes, you might just need to say it
"Hey baby, let's get it on."

# You're the One That I Want

Sometimes we meet a person whose got everything we need.
While they make you feel the healin'
they also make your heart bleed.
You feel like you go together and nothing could be wrong
singing rama lama lama ka dinga da dinga dong.
And your shoo bop sha wadda wadda yip pity boom de boom
gots your dip da dip doo wop doo da da doo bee doo.
You feel like you've finally made it all the way to the top
shaking up your chang chang changity chang sha bop.
Your heart feels like a shaken can of cherry soda pop
makes you
boogedy boogedy boogedy boogedy shooby doo wop she bop.
You know that you'd be happy to finally jump the broom
singing sha na na na na na na yippity dip de doom.
When you find that special someone
and it makes you feel all hot
those times you just gotta say it,
"Baby, you're the one that i want."

# Wonderful Tonight

Fellas, we have something to discuss.
It's about the women you love.
It's really important you appreciate them
and make them feel like they're sent from above.
For all they do for you
to make sure that you're cared for,
you need to know that they need to know
that their loved and that they are adored.
So if you want to live in harmony,
if you want your life to be colorful,
be sure to tell them how amazing they are.
Be sure to tell them they're wonderful.

# Fade Into You

I've only fallen in love one time
but that one time was for eternity.
Although I may not seem consistent,
I consistently give love earnestly.
Perhaps I don't feel like I'm enough
and need to find a partner,
someone I can give my life to
without feeling like a martyr.
Perhaps we've all been programmed
to try to find the one,
someone who will complete us
so that we can feel like we're done.
While we may actually be enough
and have nothing we really need to pursue,
we all still want to feel connection
and find someone to fade into.

# Into the Mystic

There's a place where lovers go
at the leading of their hearts
where all things come together
yet remain as separate parts.

In the portrait of life, the cacophony of sounds
falls right into harmony
and the deeper they fall in love
the more life is created artfully.

A person on their own
can create an eventful life,
but they celebrate victories alone
just as they suffer strife.

But when people come together
and hearts become as one
suffering isn't as lonely
and celebrating is a lot more fun.

For those who have found such a soul
to make life more artistic,
only they can know of the joy that abides
when you sail into the mystic.

# Despacito

We rush through life much more than we should.
We don't notice anything in our adulthood.
We're pushed to the point where we do everything fast,
but there are certain moments we'd rather have last.
The moments we most cherish, when we start to connect,
when we forget the rest of the world and start to respect
the movements of bodies and the flavor of skin,
in those beautiful moments where true love begins.
When the speed of life makes intimacy seem like its incognito,
you got and take your time, esta amor de despacito.

# I'm a Believer

It can be easy to give up on love
especially when you're alone.
You can drown yourself in misery
and make your heart like stone.
But sometimes someone comes along
and they make you feel the fever,
and where you once were filled with doubt,
they'll make you a believer.

# All Shook Up

You know what it's like to fall in love
and have your whole world rocked
by someone you think is amazing,
and when they look at you, you're shocked.
When your heart beats faster every time they're around
and sometimes when they just cross your mind,
and whenever you spend time together
every little thing in the world is just fine.
But it can be a challenge when you can't see straight
because love has filled your cup.
It's a dizzying spell to be twitterpated,
but it feels great to be all shook up.

# Nothing Compares 2 U

They say you never know what you've got
until it's already gone.
Regret for what we've let go is quite a phenomenon.
But all of us have those moments
when we feel unloved and alone,
and our minds start to recollect
the lovers we have known.
Though they may have brought us hardships
and gave us a tour of hell,
we like to forget about all those things
and just remember what was swell.
In those lonely moments
when we want love to be true
about all of our former lovers
we say nothing compares to you.

# Ain't Too Proud To Beg

When you finally find someone
with whom you have connection,
a longing in your heart,
an object for your affection,
you will go to any lengths
just to spend time near them,
and when they're not around,
you just feel off your rhythm.
And if they ever threaten
to take their love away,
we'll do everything we can to make them stay
and not be too proud to beg.

# Leaving on a Jet Plane

Goodbyes are never easy
even when they're for a short while.
You never know what life's going to bring,
whether you'll frown or smile.
We are never promised tomorrow
or any more time together.
You never know what things we'll face
or what we'll have to weather.
So be sure to love with the time that you have
and the people it contains,
and hold them tight before they leave
whether by car, by train, or jet plane.

# Raspberry Beret

Sometimes there's a woman who walks into your life
who brings you nothin' but lovin' and leaves out all the strife.
There's a magical stigma 'bout the time that you spend
havin' adventures and paintin' the town red.
She takes you outta your comfort zone and into a new one
and even while you're doin' it, you don't know what you're doin'.
If you don't know what i'm talking about
or don't know where they're at,
the girls that make memories are the ones that wear hats.

# Hippie Chick

There's a certain kinda woman for a certain kind of man.
She's don't care if her pits are shaved or if she's got a tan.
She's got a sweet aroma of musk and marijuana.
She don't celebrate Christmas, Easter, or even Hannukah.
She worships Mother Nature and don't have a full time job,
and there may be some out there who might call her a slob.
But all those guys are missin' out, I tell ya, they don't know dick
cuz they never took time to get to know
a really cool hippie chick.

# Brown Eyed Girl

Eyes are the window to the soul
and the doorway to your heart,
the place where love resides,
where good romances start.
Blue eyes are the brightest
and green can denote envy.
Hazel eyes are light and fun
but glances can be deadly.
Until you look into certain eyes,
you haven't seen the world,
for the answers to all of the mysteries of life
are in the gaze of a brown eyed girl.

# Happy

I wrote this for a woman, but there have been some others
and there'd probably be a whole lot more if I had my druthers.
There's something about 'em, the way they look, smell and taste,
and all the time I've spent with women has not been a waste.
Some have been so amazing that they've inspired songs
and they've taught me new things that I've known all along.
I've found courage I didn't know I had and selfishness I did,
and it's more often women that have shown me how to live.
You can have all your riches, and whatever strikes your fancy
but the love of a woman is what makes me most happy.

Hey babe, won't you look my way.
Look at my face,
and see the grin I got on.
Not sure how it happened there.
I don't really care,
just started up when you came along.

Got a feelin' burnin' in my soul,
makes me rock n' roll,
makes me lose control of me.
Don't care if I look a fool,
they don't think I'm cool,
I'm just as happy as I can be.

There was a time when you weren't there,
and I felt despair,
and I couldn't find my way.
You came along, grabbed a hold of me
synchronicity,
serendipity doo dah day.

I'll never be another lonely one
while we're havin' fun,
paintin' the whole town red,
green and blue. You ain't got a clue
what your smile can do,
the way it makes me lift my head.

Some people may never know
how it feels to glow,
how to let that heart light shine.
I feel so glad that we're the lucky ones,
that we're in motion,
movin' on down the line.

I got a song comin' from my heart
your life is your art,
a new canvas every day.
You're makin' something beautiful,
it's unusual,
but it makes me want to say,

Your eyes look into me,
give me what I need,
and help me to see
and your smile entices me
to be all I can be,
and all I can be is happy.

# I Second That Emotion

In this age of swipes and casual sex,
it can be hard to find connection.
It seems like everyone just wants to feel good
without knowing true affection.
While it's great to be independent
and comfortable in your own skin,
finding someone to celebrate with
improves how great it feels to win.
There's a lot to be said for intimacy,
being honest and being vulnerable.
And once you get past the hard part,
it starts to feel much more comfortable.
So if you want something more than shallow sex,
you want a love deeper than the ocean,
you might just be on to something,
and I second that emotion.

# I Love You Period

Sometimes it's hard to find the words
to express just how we're feeling,
and choosing punctuation
can sometimes leave us reeling.
How excited should we be?
Should we keep our cool?
We don't want to seem like idiots
by breaking grammatical rules.
What if we end a sentence with a preposition?
Or leave a participle dangling?
We want to use our language well
but only end up mangling
it because we try to fill our expressions with flowery words
because the ways we care are myriad,
but we'd probably be a whole lot better off
if we just said "I love you, period."

# Suddenly Seymour

Some girls, they tend to like bad boys,
ones that will boss them around.
They're okay to be treated like play toys
and get smacked without making a sound.

There ain't too much confusion
over why they feel this way.
For a long time women been losin',
been made to feel like property.

But ladies, if you've got that need
to spend all of your life with one man,
there are plenty out there that won't make you bleed.
They'll lift you up and tell you you can.

But you gotta steer clear of the bad boys
and find someone you can really adore,
preferably somebody who's gainfully employed,
a guy with a name like Seymour.

He may not be the best lookin'
or be a guy that most girls would want,
but that will keep him unremittin'
and make him appreciate the blessing he's got.

I know the bad boys are alluring,
but if you really want to be loved,
pick a lover that's much more enduring,
and makes you feel like you're sent from above.

So don't overlook the nice guys,
the ones that get picked on for being too smart.
If you're just picking lovers out because of their size,
you've already missed out from the start.

# Suspicious Minds

Trust can be rather difficult in this world in which we live,
and if you want to get it, first you gotta give,
but when half our sacred marriages end up in divorce,
when asked if he might be cheating, it's easy to say, "Of course."
If its true what the Bible says
about lust of the mind bein' the same as for real,
you can be fairly certain that every man's a heel.
But just cause we're obsessed with sex
should be no cause for alarm.
Our genital area has a mind of its own,
but it don't mean no harm.
You might just have to deal with the fact
that we often walk the line,
but it ain't gonna do you no damn good
walking around with suspicious minds.

# Love On The Rocks

You knows that feeling when a new love starts
and excitement is bursting right out of your heart.
You're happy as can be and just can't get your fill,
then eventually, things, they go downhill.
You no longer make eye contact
and when you do they burn with rage.
Where once you finally felt free, now you're in a cage.
Though love, it opens many doors, it also puts up blocks.
As high as you are when love starts,
you're as low when your love's on the rocks.

# Lovin', Touchin', Squeezin'

It's a sad affair when a lover leaves,
especially when she leaves you for somebody else,
and there's quite a bit of schadenfreude
when it happens to herself.
There's always such intensity when you're able to love another.
You always learn about yourself when find yourself a lover.
But when it's gone, and they always end,
you're no longer lovers and no longer friends,
tryin to find the pieces to your shattered puzzled heart,
as positive as you wanna be, all you feel is dark.

# Why Did I Chase You Away?

There's something about a country song.
They're obliged to say how we've done it all wrong.
Something about bein' poor and all that you lose,
the white man's version of singin' the blues.
But of all the things we may have lost,
our truck, our dog, our dental floss,
there ain't nothin' as bad as losin' a love
and knowin it was you that made her run off.

There were days when a letter
could only say it better
if my tears learned how to write.
There were nights that I held you
reached out and I felt you
turn away and face the night.

There were holes in my pockets
sold my soul to stop it
watched my dreams burn fire bright.
I recall my ever after
as I climbed Jacob's Ladder
and everything turned out right.

Happy young lovers
need only each other
and hope to keep sorrow at bay.
Years take their toll
as we slowly grow old
and young love passes away.

I gave up on my dreams
and I fashioned my schemes
to get by from day to day.
You were always beside me
but I made it unlikely
to be a man who could get you to stay.

Why do I realize the good that I had
after it's all done and gone?
Why do I realize the right thing to do
after I've done it all wrong?
If only tomorrow were yesterday
I'd let you know just how much you belong
You're all I've ever needed or had
and you were right there with me all along.

Why ain't today
the way it looked when I saw it yesterday?
Tomorrow looks darker
when seen in the light of today.
Where did my dreams go
when I woke up alone in reality?
Where did you go?
And why did I chase you away?

# I'm So Lonesome I Could Cry

Alone, lonely, and lonesome
are various degrees
of being by yourself
from peaceful to disease.
Being alone is one thing.
You may love your company.
You're fine with being on your own
and don't need anybody.
Lonely is where the pain sets in
and there are people that you miss.
You wish you could be with them
and you start to feel distress.
But taking it even deeper
where you almost want to die,
lonesome is as bad as it can get
when you're so lonesome you just want to cry.

# Romeo & Juliet

We've got this romantic notion
about lovin for life it seems.
We're lookin for the potion
that'll give us what we need.

Though marriage started as a business trade,
we got all doey-eyed about it,
and all the ceremony we went and made
makes us almost blow a gasket.
Signin' up for a full time lover
gives you semi-regular access to sex,
but you can't have another
or you'll end up as an ex.

It's a peculiar situation,
this here monogamy.
It's the crux of civilization,
but it ain't worked out for me.

It's true I like to wander
and I have been known to flirt,
and I can't help but wonder
what's up everybody's skirt.

Though some may die for true love
and may try to find "the one",
my cynicality has made me tired of
hopin' for love and a settin' sun.
Star crossed lovers are pretty sad,
this much I know is true.
I'll settle for a one night stand.
You up for it? How 'bout you?

# THE WANDERING SOUL

With his penchant to hit the trail and go beyond the horizon, the cowboy is a bit of a wanderer. This is where The Eagles had their idea for "Desperado" and what I felt when I was traveling and wrote my song "On The Road". While U2 may have touched upon the cowboy's state with "I Still Haven't Found What I'm Looking For", in actuality, the search is what the cowboy is searching for.

Often misunderstood by traditionalists and puritans, the cowboy does sometimes cry out "The Prodigal's Lament", call out for partners in crime as Amy Winehouse did with "Valerie", and does have a little concern about going "Straight To Hell" just like Drivin' and Cryin'.

But ultimately, like John Prine, the cowboy would prefer to be an "Angel from Montgomery", and because some do consider him crazy for the life he leads, like Billy Joel, the cowboy merely tips his hat and says "You May Be Right".

# Desperado

There's a certain kind of wanderer
who won't come in from the cold.
Though some think he's an idiot, he thinks he's pretty bold.
He's tryin to find his way alone, on the range and on the sea
and he's got a bit of an aversion to being in community.
That streak of independence upon which this land was founded
forces him to go it alone so he can go get grounded.
But it ain't alone that we find ourselves,
regardless of our bravado.
It's in the eyes of those we love, ya dumb ass desperado.

# On the Road

Took off for California, made it halfway there,
blizzards took my roads away and left me snowblind.
It's a permanent vacation for the next few months,
just waitin' for that snow to melt
in that rocky mountain sunshine,
then i'll be on the road again.
They say it's my way of thinkin' that keeps me seekin' more.
Some say my wires are wrapped too loosely,
some say I've come unwound.
Somewhere in Carolina, the future passed me by.
All my dreams were blinked away,
I think they headed westbound
so I took to the road again.
There's Tao between reflectors, Nirvana's exit fifty three,
even my man Jesus said "take up your cross and follow me."
I put it in my backpack right next to my canteen.
I was hoping for some living water, got crucifixion tea.
I found it on the road again.

Some miles last for minutes.
Some inches last for days.
Only two choices at a fork in the road,
where's your imagination?
Cars were meant to hurry,
planes were meant to rush.
I'm thinking about the journey,
I reached my destination
when I took to the road again.
Soon I'll be on the road again.

# I Still Haven't Found What I'm Lookin' For

To say I'm a wanderer wouldn't be too far off.
I've been called a lot worse. It's part of the job.
They've called me dreamer, searcher and vagabond too.
But it's not what I am, it's just what I do.
I look for life's intricacies and the way they show up,
seeking out synchronicities to fill up my cup.
Some folks like security and a home with a door,
but I ain't yet found what I'm lookin for.

# The Prodigal's Lament

My mother used to tell me that I was the prodigal son.
It would appear that I've done everything I could
to live up to that definition.
I've squandered my youth on idiocy,
spent my money on experience.
I haven't been too stern
and I haven't been too serious.
I've taken life one day at a time
and haven't worried about tomorrow.
That's brought its share of blessed moments
and brought its share of sorrow.
Though some may look at me as the poster child
for a life that has been wasted,
I'm still grateful for the path I've taken
and the life that I've created.
Though I may not be perfect
and may be considered a prodigal,
it's worked for me to not be religious
but just to be philosophical.

I've got nothing in common with my brother,
a father of two in a god-fearin' home.
Should I have a family? Why bother?
I find a home wherever I roam.
I look to my sins for forgiveness,
for reason, I look to my doubt.
I look to my bad to find goodness,
sometimes you gotta give in to find out.
Now Jesus, he didn't like no preachers,
that's a sentiment I can often relate,
and as good as he was as a teacher,
I've learned much more from all my mistakes.
I've learned a valuable lesson
about judging before hearing a plea.
Jesus was right about one thing,
sinners make great company.
So as my feet dangle in the chasm,
and I rest my head right on the edge,
blind faith has found me some footholds,
and all of my detours have come to a bridge.

I like cream in my coffee. I like sweet in my tea.

I like Jack in my cola,

and my favorite cigarettes are rolled up with weed.

Mama, can you see right through me

when I say that heaven can wait?

I know Jesus will leave a light on for me

cuz he knows that I'm always late.

But mama will you forgive me

when I do what you don't understand?

Your innocent dreamer of a bright blue eyed boy

has become a passionate man.

# Valerie

There once was a girl named Amy
who got herself into some trouble.
She lived her life in the fast lane
as if she lived in a bubble.
And some of us live just like her
but only from time to time,
and when there are shenanigans to be gotten into,
we always have a partner in crime.
But this partner can't be just anyone,
someone from the peanut gallery.
Our accomplice must be someone special,
someone just like Valerie.

# Straight to Hell

I've faltered quite a bit
as I've tried to walk the straight and narrow,
though I must admit,
I've never tried to be as straight as an arrow.
I've lived my life the best I could
and tried to be of service,
however, when it comes to common sense,
I've often been impervious.
Ever since I was a little boy,
I've been told I was a sinner,
and if they handed out prizes for achieving that goal,
I'd certainly be a winner.
It's not that I try to be bad,
and do things that are wrong.
I just walk to the beat of a different drummer
and sing a different song.
But even through all of my blunder
things are still working out well,
but there's still a part of me that wonders
if I'm going straight to hell.

# Angel From Montgomery

There are all sorts of things I've wanted to be,
goals that I've wanted to reach.
There's been times I wanted a fancy car
and a great big house on the beach.
I've wanted to be a world changer,
and I've wanted to see the world change.
Trying to be so many things
can make you feel sort of strange.
But the world is indeed changing
and there's more opportunity
to reach the goals you set for yourself
as crazy as they may be.
I've been tempted to be a lot of things
so I could reach my potential,
but if the good lord makes me anything,
I hope he one day makes me an angel.

# You May Be Right

Insanity is doing the same thing over and over
and expecting different results.
Crazy's a whole lot simpler.
It just means you're kinda nuts.
People look down upon it
and say that you're mentally ill,
but it's the crazy ones who bring flavor to life
and give us that little thrill.
Always pushin' the boundaries
and always ridin' the the line,
it's the crazy ones who get us out of our box
so we don't all lose our minds.
When you say the world is goin' mad,
you may very well be right,
but say a prayer for those crazy folk,
they're the ones shinin' the light.

# BLAZING THE TRAIL

Although he may be crazy, the cowboy is necessary. In his desire to blaze new trails, he takes Xavier Rudd's advice to "Follow The Sun" and agrees with Kermit the Frog that we will someday find "The Rainbow Connection". He wants to let those he loves know that "Life Is Better With You" as Michael Franti does, and he wants them to "Feel" how much they are loved.

The cowboy blazes the trails he does because he shares the sentiment that "We Shall Be Free" with Garth Brooks and knows that part of it is realizing that we are all "One" just like U2 did. To do that, like Nick Lowe, we need to ask "What's So Funny About Peace, Love & Understanding?"

The challenge the cowboy feels is that not all heroes are all they're cut out to be, and some are just as "Lost As Me". After all, not all heroes accept the responsibility that comes with their power like "Spider Man" does but part of that responsibility is to listen to the advice from "Dear Abby" via John Prine and be thankful for what we have. For the one constant in life is change, and as Bob Dylan reminds us now in every generation, "The Times They Are A'Changin'".

Of course, the cowboy's world view is changing as well. He doesn't think much of dogma and appreciates the simplicity of

Ziggy Marley's claim that "Love Is My Religion". He believes that if Jesus were to come back, he'd be a simple servant like in James Corbin's song "Waffle House Jesus".

The cowboy doesn't give much credence to having it all figured out, and, like the Indigo Girls, he feels that he's "Closer To Fine" when he's not looking for definitives. But he does realize the power of forgiveness and would like to see more religious folk answer the call to "Forgive Me" that comes from so many who are punished on various levels, which explains why he is "Losing My Religion" with REM.

But the cowboy does identify with his Creator, and will sing "Hallelujah" along with Leonard Cohen, even if he isn't dogmatic. Because the cowboy knows that the truth of life is beyond religion and his spirits, he asks that his Creator "Reveal It In Me." In order to truly blaze the trails that will guide us to the tomorrow we seek, we have to shine our "True Colors" just like Cyndi Lauper and listen to "The Sound of Sunshine" along with Michael Franti.

# Follow the Sun

With all the stuff going on in this here civilization
it ain't infrequent to lose our direction.
All the gizmos and gadgets, they want your attention,
advertisements on all the billboards and benches.
Everything's important to somebody or another
and with all of the noise you can feel yourself smothered.
When you've lost your direction and your long day is done
you'll always find clarity when you follow the sun.

# The Rainbow Connection

A wise frog once said it weren't easy to be green
and although I'm more off white, I know what he means.
It feels strange to be the oddball
and stand out cuz you're different.
Sometimes you feel like you're way too deficient.
Everybody else has a purpose and place
and sometimes you feel like you're from outer space.
We highlight our differences and classifications
into all races and creeds, classes and nations,
but beyond all our variances and reasons to fraction,
someday we'll find it, the rainbow connection.

# Life Is Better With You

Though we have this thing called social media
we're still rather anti-social,
and our technology has now become so advanced
that communication has gotten global.
But we're still not that good with engagement
and many people still feel left out.
A lot of us suffer from loneliness
and are filled with all sorts of doubt
whether or not we're worth anything
if we have anything to offer,
but if we want the world that we've dreamed of,
if we really want to prosper,
we've got to let those people know
through word, through action, and letter
that life is still worth living
and that they make our lives so much better.

# *Feel*

Sometimes life can be sad
and there are times we could all use some soothing.
We don't always get all the comfort we want
at least not by our own choosing.
And when those we love really need us
sometimes we just can't be found
so love them for all you're worth when you're with them
so they can still feel it when you're not around.

You lie in bed and you stare up at the ceiling.
Your whole life is reeling
and you just can't get control.
Every day, you give more than you're given.
You feel like you've been driven right into a hole.
Love, love has left you tattered,
your heart has been so shattered,
and your peace is all in pieces.
You're out of strength, and all you feel is weakness.
Your world is full of bleakness,
and your hope only decreases.
This world can be so unforgiving.
You work hard to make a living,
just trying to make ends meet,
and you pull, no matter how tightly
it just seems so unlikely
that you'll overcome defeat.
You try, but you just keep getting smacked down
as you fade into the background
and your dreams they fade to dust.
Once, your eyes they shined so brightly
but now your future looks unsightly
as your wants gave way to musts.

Though you, you just cannot see it,
I can't help but believe it,
you've got a spirit in you
that lives just to pull you through.
When you're feeling all alone,
when your energy is gone,
when you're aching to your bones,
I hope you feel me.
When you've got nothing more to give,
your path has brought you to a cliff,
when it takes all you've got to live,
I hope you feel me.
When you can't take another step,
and you're shooting from the hip,
when life just gives you lip,
I hope you feel me.
When you need to find some strength,
when you're looking for your place,
when you need someone to have faith in you,
just feel me,
Feel me loving you.

# We Shall Be Free

It's a difficult thing to find the solutions
to problems that we've made ourselves.
It's often rather tempting
to stash our hopes up on the shelves.

We are a crazy species
us homo sapiens.
While we are a pretty creative bunch
it'd be great if we could make amends
for all our brilliant fervor
and things that we have done.
It's a might bit disconcertin'
the things we've done for fun.
We've cordoned off our imaginary lines
of real estate and borders
to ensure that somewhere each of us
is an alien interloper.

We've enslaved ourselves to serving those
who only serve themselves.
We find every reason we can to fight
but far too few to help.

You'd think for all our ingenuity
we'd find a better way,
but we're too concerned with who's shtoopin' who
and what celebutantes have to say.
But I'm still somehow hopeful
from the leaders I have seen
that if we just remember how to love
we can all be free.

# One

As we've gone and developed the world that we know
we've taken some liberties and put on quite a show
by building society through hacking it up
into races, creeds, teams, and all sorts of dogma.
We love setting boundaries and building up borders.
We love feeling superior by dishing out orders.
Yet beyond all our excitement to make the world in our image
there's a bit of an issue with how we've set up our visage.
We tend to think that those sharing our world
are just a bunch of others
but the truth is all of us,
every one, are sisters and brothers.
We feel safe thinking we're separate
when we let our flags unfurl,
but the truth is we're all one,
one life, one love, one world.

# What's So Funny 'Bout Peace, Love & Understanding?

If you're a spectator of life like I am
you got plenty of reason to laugh.
We're a species of primarily idiots
who turn everything into trash.
This circus we call a government
is nothin' but a joke.
They offer up the American Dream
but dreams just turn to smoke.
Now not everybody's laughin'
at all the trouble that we make,
when everything ends up broken
when we finally get a break.
There's a few things we needn't laugh about
as we fully feel the rub.
For instance, I can't find what's funny
about understanding, peace and love.

# Lost As Me

We have this weird way of worshipping heroes
and now with the internet, they all come up zeroes.
And we're greatly offended when the mighty have fallen
and those we looked up to have proved to be human.
There's a good chance our heroes of old weren't much better
but news travelled slower when all you had was a letter.
In the digital age, we all know it all now
when somebody screws up and lets us all down.
It should make us wonder when we're choosing our idols
if they deserve all the credit they may get with their titles.
The truth is we're all just finding our way.
Though we're all lost together, we'll get there someday.

Batman's a gray-haired loony, Superman is dead
Spider Man got married, Slick Willie's getting head.
My pastor's got a golden tooth, my deacon's got a whore,
and if a priest touches a kid again, we'll show 'em holy war.

You want more coin for playing baseball or you won't play at all
while I make eight fifty an hour and the boss has got my balls.
Will hands that caught a football fit into a glove?
Should this be the way we all should say goodbye to love?

My home state's got hanging chads, now they've hung us all.
How can Bush stretch his trigger finger? Just give old dad a call.
America, America, sweet home of the brave,
let's lock up all those brown skinned boys
just to keep us white boys safe.
Now we've got Obamacare, change hope, yes, we can.
Give the prick a Nobel prize and he's dropping bombs again.

Where is the man on the white horse?
Where is the hero in the mask?
How's anybody gonna help me
when they're all too busy covering their ass?

All my heroes are long gone.
They all let me down.
The sheriff just left town.
Can I look up to anyone?
Is it all an illusion?
Or is everybody just as lost as me?

# Spider Man

For most kids I know, their favorite moments
are watching cartoons and reading comic books.
And of all of the heroes that I've seen on the screen
with their bulging pectorals and spandex everything,
there was one of those guys I could really connect with.
He was kind of a smart ass which some say I act as,
but he's a down to earth guy
when he's not swinging from towers,
and he said responsibility comes with great power.
While he was only a drawing, he meant much more to me.
We all got our heroes that we wanna be.
So you take your Captain America, Superman and the Bat.
I'll stick with Spider Man. That dude knows where it's at.

# Dear Abby

Though we often get caught up in home runs and goal lines,
it would seem that complaining is our favorite past time.
The gummint does this, and our neighbor did that.
Everyone's stupid and everything makes us fat.
Wherever we can, we bitch, whine, and moan,
and just can't understand why we go home alone.
We reach out to others for commiseration
but we'd do a lot better if we'd just quit complainin'.

# The Times They Are a'Changin'

It's an amazing time we live in, the things that we get to see.
We're advanced in all our warfare and new technology.
But all these little gadgets that help us communicate
are for more than battlin' pokemons
and finding more reasons to hate.
While machines can't make the changes that truly need to be,
they offer us the chance to change and opportunity.
So if we want to use this particular time and place
to put down all our gizmos and look each other in the face
we'll find the change we're looking for ain't in technology.
If we really wanna change the world, we gotta change me to we.

# Love Is My Religion

Some choose to worship and kneel down to pray,
ask God for forgiveness for being this way,
the way that He made us, or it coulda been She
but somehow we think we're not what we should be.
Now I don't really go in for that dogma hubbub.
If you wanna ask me, my religion is love.

# Waffle House Jesus

If Jesus were to come back now
I think he'd take a menial job.
He wouldn't be a vagabond
and he wouldn't be a slob.
I think he would take a position
where he could be of service
not to the elite who run things now
but somewhere for the rest of us.
He wouldn't bring an end to the world
but an end to the way that we see it.
Though people might ask him for change,
he would encourage them to be it.
He wouldn't run for president
or try to make everything lawful.
He'd probably just try to spread love around,
and he'd probably be making waffles.

# Closer to Fine

It seems there's a whole a lot of people
who say that they've got the secret of life,
and though they say that they're all kinds of peaceful,
they still seem wracked with strife.
Some of them have holy books
chock full of all the answers.
Quite a few are nothin but crooks
and around the truth they're dancers.
For all those who say they have the one true way
and are touched by the divine,
the less I heed what they have to say,
the closer I am to fine.

# Forgive Me

We've all got our stories, the things that we've faced.
Some have ended in victory and some in disgrace.
We all choose our rights, and we all choose our wrongs.
Our biggest mistake is dragging others along.
Holding up others to the standard we set
is setting ourselves up for a lot of regret.
Instead of morality telling them how to live,
we'd do a lot better learning how to forgive.

I meant to drop a dime but I dropped twenty.
It ain't no loss, you can't smoke money.
They say it can't buy happiness, I beg to differ, I confess,
I do what I need and I need to cope,
sucking bottles and smoking dope.
You hold my weakness as my sin,
that explains the bind we're in.
Will you forgive me so I can forgive myself?
Will you show your God to me,
or will you hide him in the book there on your shelf?

She was the first in her family to get this far,
and what she is is what you are.
Ten credits to go 'til she was done,
nine months until she had his son.
He turned his back and left her alone,
and each day since she's had to atone.
Fingers point and whispers hush,
all she asks, she don't ask much,
will you forgive me so I can forgive myself?
Will you show your God to me,
or will you hide him in the book there on your shelf?

I cannot find the love in me if you cannot find it in you.
Will you represent your God to me?
Do you offer faith and hope and love as fruit?


Uncle Jack smiled when he was ten,
an innocent tickle was how it began.
Bring up your child in the way he should go,
cause what he's taught is what he knows.
Where love was offered, love is found
and what goes around has come around.
Will you tell him that his tune is wrong
when he finally feels a song?
Will you forgive me, so I can forgive myself?
Can you see your God in me,
an abomination by that book upon your shelf?

Turn your head on the man with the cardboard sign
who feeds his kids on nursery rhymes.
"No good begger, get a job" well, he's got a door, but got no knob,
and to give him a buck is to feed the plague,
but so much healing from one band aid.
What's a fallen man to do, cry to God, cry out to you?
Will you forgive me so I can forgive myself?
Will you show your God to me,
or is he hidden in that book there on your shelf?

I take full blame for what I have become.
My foolish ways
have made me come undone.
But how long
must my punishment survive?
My blood still flows, but I'm barely alive.
And only when you see your God in me
will He make His grace
shine through you.
I'm trying to be
what He's calling me to be,
through the least of us, He is calling you.

# Losing My Religion

There are some who say that God
can only be found in the Bible,
and they keep prayin' and yellin'
for some kind of big revival,
but I've got some real big issues
with some of their holy doctrines,
and there seems to be some discrepancies
'tween their message and their actions.
Since it serves as the central crux
of all our western culture,
we got the right to ask some questions
when their story seems peculiar.
They're welcome to try to limit God to sixty six books
and keep givin their money to fakers and crooks,
but when they start tellin' me I gotta live by their rules
I got an obligation to tell 'em they're fools.
For one, they got this claim that their book is flawless
and if you don't believe it, it's cuz you're so lawless.
You don't have a choice, and they say you can't pick and choose,
but there's just so much bullshit that they still always do.

Though there were more than a hundred accounts
of this dude they called Jesus,
they got narrowed down to four
cuz all the others were blasphemous.
Then they shoved in thirteen letters
from some dude Jesus never met.
He was the coat check boy at the first martyrdom
and a big misogynist.
Then you gotta lug all these laws from generation to generation,
but nobody follows those rules or abstains from abominations.
I get their need to feel secure
and have something to believe in,
but when they can't use no damn common sense
and won't listen to reason
I feel compelled to point out all the flaws in their age-old story,
this idea of a God who made all this just to get some glory.
He made us humans being and gave us all free will
but didn't have the foresight to see how that'd go downhill?
If he knew we'd all have to go to hell
if we didn't polish the pews
I think he'd come up with something better
than such a violent form of good news.
This story of God that we've all heard may just be a bit contrived
after all, history's written by the stories that survive.

I think God's much bigger
than the character in that biblical box,
and destructive ideas
have spread like the plague
or maybe chicken pox.
The dogma other men hold to
feels to me too much like a prison,
but I feel a heck of a lot freer now
that I've done gone and lost
my old religion.

# Hallelujah

If you pay any sort of attention
you can't help but to be thankful
and when you are, you see life provides
from each and every angle.
We're given bodies to do stuff and feel good,
breaths to breathe all the day through,
and support to achieve our endeavors
in most everything we do.
Although society says everything's scarce,
there's abundance if you know how to see,
and every challenge we face
becomes opportunity.
Sometimes we just have to say thank you
to Jesus, Allah, or the Buddha,
to whatever it is that keeps giving us life,
we can't help but say hallelujah.

# Reveal It In Me

I do believe in God
but I'm not sure what it is.
I don't think it's a he or a she,
a mister or a miz,
but I know it's given me every breath
and it just keeps on giving,
empowering me with what I need
so I can go on living.
And since I'm so well provided for
by the Creator of all that I know,
I'm grateful for what I'm given
by the Source of all that flows.
And while I can't give it a name
or articulate what I believe,
it feels like the power of love,
and I pray it reveals it in me.

Much easier to be a poet than a saint,
give my mind to spirits instead of pray.
I sing the blues to chase my sorrows away
instead of rising without mournin' every day.
But my spirits have all failed me,
brought as much ease as pain.
The mistakes that helped create me
taught me enough to say,
that can't be you, I feel it in me.
Teach me to listen and help me to see.
Awaken my faith more than my belief.
Reveal your truth, Lord, reveal it in me.
When we choose to follow, we choose to lead,
and take another pilgrim's journey when we read.
Eat another's fruit and we plant a seed,
and we run from all the ghosts we've never seen.
Whose footsteps do I follow
stained with ink and blood and wine?
Am I standin' in my brother's tracks or does he walk in mine?
As we trample on your hallowed ground lookin' 'til we're blind
a still small voice is whispering in the corner of my mind

That can't be you, I feel it in me.

Teach me to listen and help me to see.

Awaken my faith more than my belief.

Reveal your truth, Lord, reveal it in me.

The way that my mind scurries from dream to dream,

be it waking nightmare, ritual, or scheme,

forever momentary, I can see

that this is all of you and part of me.

When my eyes are open and your breath is there,

when faith returns to mystery and I believe without a care,

what I don't know won't hurt me and I have known despair,

and everyone watched over me cuz you were always there.

It's all of you, I feel it in me.

Teach me to listen, you taught me to see.

Awaken my faith more than my beliefs.

Reveal your truth, Lord, reveal it in me.

# True Colors

There's a lot that we do to hide who we are.
We shore up our egos to keep people afar.
We're never quite sure about who we can trust
and there's very few times we can truly be us.
We're all so caught up in puttin' up pretense
that we often miss out on life because we're playing defense.
but if you can see past all the bullshit and bluster,
you'll fare a lot better if you just shine your true colors.

# *The Sound of Sunshine*

There's a beautiful thing about the place where i'm from.
It's called Sarasota and its a whole lot of fun.
We're known for our beaches and beautiful women,
retirement villages and people with millions.
We get a bad rap for mistreating the homeless
and get caught up in politics so we can call ourselves blameless.
We could do much better, that much is true
and the call we should heed tells us just what to do,
but until we can hear it, when we're in our right minds,
we're just sitting here listenin' to the sound of sunshine.

# BEYOND THE HORIZON

Because he seeks what's beyond the horizon, the cowboy looks beyond the status quo. When he looks at mainstream society, he stands with 4 Non Blondes and asks "What's Up?". He recognizes that "Political Science" is no science at all and should be satirized like Randy Newman.

He also sings along with Johnny Cash on the "Folsom Prison Blues" due to the number of people we now have imprisoned and bemoans the "Mad World" we've created with Tears for Fears. Prince reminds him that all of our incessant arguing sounds like it does "When Doves Cry" and that all of our "Isms are Schisms" that only serve to separate us while the people who run the isms take full advantage.

In seeking the answers to a better way, he asks, along with Pink, "What About Us?" as he seeks a way to "Fix You" along with Coldplay. Looking at the insanity of the world makes him want to join Lyle Lovett on the sea "If I Had A Boat" because like Izzy pointed out, "Somewhere Over The Rainbow" we'll be able to see "What A Wonderful World" it is.

But to actually get beyond the horizon, we've got to stand with Ben Harper and start to believe in a "Better Way". While getting there may seem like a "Long Crawl", to watch how society is moving now is, as John Lennon put it, just like "Watching The Wheels".

# What's Up?

There's a lot going on in this day and age
that makes some of us rejoice and some of us rage.
If you're caught in the mainstream
you might find yourself numb,
if you're outside the current, you think everyone's dumb.
It's true that a lot of us follow like lemmings,
jumping to our death based on others condemnings.
We're all so caught up in listening to others,
we release common sense
and what we learned from our mothers.
This thing we call money is just so pervasive
and heeding its call can make true joy evasive.
All wrapped up in this art form and the debt it creates
makes us focused on ledgers and not how we relate.
We now call on rich folk to help us escape our distress
but the big challenge there is that they're the sickest.
However, we keep on fighting wars
so they can keep making their profits
while we should ask, "What's up?"
and stop acting like puppets.

# Political Science

The challenge with being American is you have to be the best
seems like every sort of move we make
is some kind of cosmic test.
Though some countries are better
at healthy living, math, and science,
the USA's got more explosives
and can bomb them all into compliance.

Though few of us want so much carnage
and would rather just go our way,
for many, pride is the highest of virtues
and they insist that honor is paid.

Some feel that we're the policemen
and our military keeps the world safe,
but some fear we're the world's bullies
and would rather we refrain.

The biggest challenge
we have right now,
the volatility of our situation,
is that a tweet could be offensive
to the temporary chief of our nation.
Flared egos can be fragile
and need to be treated well,
especially when that dainty little ego
can blow the world to hell.

# Folsom Prison Blues

There once was a man in black
who would often walk the line.
He was the first to play in prison
a place the world was blind.
Considering our new model
of makin money from incarceration
seems there should be a lot more songs
popping up around the nation.
But nobody sings about life inside.
Most of us, we'd rather just run and hide.
But while the imprisoned just don't make the news
the best that we got's the Folsom Prison Blues.

# Mad World

If you guys ain't noticed, this world has gone mad.
We're faced with all kinds of troubles that we've never had.
It seems like with every advance or innovation,
we just make things more complexer with more complications.
We're workin our asses off just to make rent,
and collectors are callin' for our healthcare payment.
We're caught in a rat race and there ain't no damn cheese,
and each day we feel like we're brought to our knees.
Whether were prayin or whether we're blowin',
no matter how far we go, we never get where we're goin'.
Maybe someday the world won't seem so damn mad,
but in the meantime, it's really damn sad.

# When Doves Cry

These days, we like to argue
about anything we can.
Whether we prefer red or blue,
Democrat or Republican.
But we're not supposed to fight this much,
and most of our arguments are fabricated,
and while we are fighting amongst one another
some just laugh at the mess they've created.
But hopefully, we can find some connection
and get to the heart of who, what, where, and why.
Until then, all of this bickering
sounds just like it does when doves cry.

# Isms Are Schisms

Isms are schisms, that's just what they are.
They look at what's near to get to what's far.
Of Capital, Commune, Social, or Nihil,
they all help to guide us toward ideas on trial.

Isms are schisms, they condense and divide.
Bonds get tight and chasms get wide.
By thinking together, we develop our culture.
Whatever we make, we devour like vultures.

Isms are schisms, they put us into classes.
They keep us in boxes and make us all act like asses.
Whatever your ism, you've got to go deeper,
beyond all of our differences and all our agreements.

Isms are schisms, ideas are ideals.
Words are just symbols and emotions are feels.
They are all just tools to help us become who we are.
We can use them to create and we can use them to spar.

If you use an ism to carve out your ego,
it could be a help, a hindrance,
or even placebo.
The question's not really
which ism is right
and will prove to the world
who has the most might.
Beyond all our isms
and the ways they divide us,
the question's who you are
and how you'll inspire us.

# What About Us?

From the time we first established kingdoms,
we've had our hierarchies,
and the fact that we still support them now
some would call malarkey.

Our first kings were revered
because they prevailed in battle.
Unfortunately that meant a lot of other people
were treated no better than cattle.

As the bloodlines of royal lineage
grew thicker, slower, and fatter,
what happened to the common folk
just didn't seem to matter.

As the game of thrones unraveled
and kingdoms became corporations,
the battles won by those at the top
were largely selfish exploitations.

Now we're at a point where almost all that we do
goes to the regal heirs at the top,
and because they were born learning to suck,
they're never going to stop.

So before they absorb everything,
there's something we need to discuss.
Instead of supporting these kings with no scars,
we should be asking, "what about us?"

# Fix You

Many of us feel like we're broken.
Our society has made us all crack.
We finally succumbed to the burden
of carrying it all on our backs.
We've experienced emotional trauma,
and some have physical scars.
We've been inundated with bad ideas
and feel like we're behind bars.
We all want someone to heal us,
someone to help pull us through.
I'm still trying to get my own shit together.
How the hell am I supposed to fix you?

# If I Had a Boat

When you look around at what's going on
it can make you pretty sad.
Whether you think you're on the right or the left,
you feel like you been had.

We're not really sure which way is up
or how things got this way,
but it seems that everything has just gone to shit
and someone's gotta pay.

And it's usually up to the common folk
to ante up and foot the bill
while the people who actually have money
are safe upon their hill.

They tell us what to think about
through their papers and tv stations
to ensure that we'll be fighting each other
all across the nation.

Some of us would rather stay out
of their manufactured conflict,
and when it all will end
none of us can predict.

Seems like every day
it's just getting more cut throat,
and you can bet your ass I'd just sail away
if I only had a boat.

# Somewhere Over The Rainbow / What A Wonderful World

We like to use our imaginations
as we think of the way things could be.
We dream of far-off places
where everyone is free.
Sometimes we entertain magic
and hope for the gold at the end of rainbows.
For some reason, this world just isn't enough
and there's a better way, we suppose.
But when you really look around
at how things have unfurled,
it really is a beautiful life
and it's a truly wonderful world.

# Better Way

We got our way of doin' things
and some think that it's workin'
while most of us have the sneakin'
suspicion that it's broken.
While the rich get richer,
and the poor get poorer,
and the rest of us are shown
our way to the door,
we're all in it alone
sufferin' together,
givin' our everything
to those who don't know no better.
Every two years we get something to say
but someday we'll find there's a much better way.

# Long Crawl

For the man who has a vision
for the way things could be done
it's an awfully long damn journey
until the race is run.
It seems so clear in our minds
just how things should be
but gettin' folks to go along
is harder than it seems.
You look around at suff'rin'
and you look around at lack,
and though you want to show folks how to shed it all
you carry it all on your back.
And while you don't quite feel
like you're up against a wall,
to get to where you wanna be
it's an awfully long damn crawl.

Wise man said to be the change you want to see,
the change you want to see in your world.
Hopeless is the man who tries to bother me
by setting fire to what has been unfurled.

The beginning is the end for all eternity,
and each new day brings the death of one day old.
Building on these moments that my eyes have seen,
looking down the cold and lonely road.

Yesterday was tomorrow only the day before.
I watched it pass through my hooded eyes.
What kind of man has never watched the sunset?
What kind of man has never longed to fly?

Faithless is the man who never takes a step
toward the horizon where he stores his dreams.
You'll never fly if you don't take that running start
and you'll never soar if you don't spread your wings.

You never know what's behind that golden door
and you won't get in if you don't have the key.
You push and push until you cannot try no more.
You grunt, you sweat, you ache, you hurt, you bleed.

Givin' up comes easy for the weaker man,
lyin' down comes easy for the dead,
comfort finds the man who strives to stand his ground
leaning on the shoulders of his friends.

It's a long crawl from where I am to where I want to be
and it's a far cry from what I feel to what I let you see.

# Watching the Wheels

There are some who hold it against me
that I just don't give a shit
'bout what the hell you do with your flag
or your fancy government.
I think it's just a lot of noise
to make more than nessec'ry happen
and it may just be the drama
that makes it so attractin'.
I'd rather stick to myself and the people I know
and trust that we'll work it out.
I got no need to play the games
most people worry about.
So you get caught up in your races and games
and all of your really big deals.
I'll be just fine spendin' my own time
just sittin' here watchin' the wheels.

# THE PATH TO FREEDOM

Nearly more than any other thing, the cowboy loves his freedom, and because he has it, he longs to share it with others. He knows how good it feels to "Breathe" free, and he knows that many others feel like Queen and scream, "I Want To Break Free". However, the true cowboy isn't the slave to tobacco that the Marlboro Man makes him out to be, and he has sung his "Sweet Leaf Serenade" in order to breathe more easily.

Like Gavin Degraw, the cowboy wants to be "Free" and feel the wind in his hair, and like Tom Petty, he realizes that sometimes freedom is "Free Fallin'". And sometimes, as George Michael put it in "Freedom 90", freedom is about taking lies and making them true.

Part of finding our path to freedom is understanding the limits that we face, like the limits of our language and how often we limit ourselves by how we use it with phrases like "If Only". But life isn't always fair, and Frank Sinatra reminds us that "That's Life". It's a "Wild World" just like Cat Stevens said, and "You Can't Always Get What You Want" as the Rolling Stones pointed out.

However, life still does provide, and part of our freedom lies in not wanting as much. The cowboy sees a lot of wisdom in the animals he encounters, especially the ones who sing about "The Bare Necessities". For although the game of "Venery" has given groups of animals all sorts of complicated names, when we realize that "I Don't Need Anything That I Don't Have" like Glen Philips, we're often a lot better off.

Where we can find our true treasures are in "The People That Made Me", from "Danny Boy" on to those with whom you and Ed Sheeran may have watched the sun set from a "Castle On A Hill".

Ultimately, the cowboy, like the Zen monk, helps us realize that to enjoy life and find our freedom, we must "Be Here Now" and be grateful for "Every Little Thing".

# Breathe

In the society we are creating,
we're under quite a bit of pressure
to meet the demands of others
and make sure that we measure
up to all that is expected
to be a good consumer
and though we're often pushed to our limits,
we try to do it with good humor.
But it seems that all our consumption
just serves to keep us busy,
and the speed in which we create pollution and trash
can make us rather dizzy.
I know that I'm supposed to step in line
so the masters can be appeased,
but I don't see the point in this mayhem.
I just want to breathe.

Freedom used to mean something before it was taken away.
We sacrificed the oceans and we sacrificed the bay.
We treat our Mother Nature as badly as we treat ourselves,
making profits for the big boys and giving up our health.

But the poison, it keeps flowing.
Gotta keep their numbers growing
they think we somehow owe them everything.
But I'd rather have my time back
and a whole lot fewer smokestacks
and avoid all of the heart attacks they bring.

There was a time that we were better at appreciating life.
Somewhere along our way, we opted for more strife.
We sell our time, our everything
to pay the people who now own
all the places we like to go and stare into our phones.

But the money must keep flowing
the debt it must keep growing
and all because we owe them, we're property.
But I can't afford my healthcare
cuz we need more corporate welfare.
There oughtta be a ban on billionaires and greed.

Everyone wants something
and some want everything.
Even all the poorest folks think they should be kings.
We kill ourselves off slowly with fast food, hate and stress.
Most of us get it worst of all cuz we gotta be the best.
Gotta keep on making progress.
Gotta get that bigger office.
Gotta sieze every opportunity.
The rat race keeps us running
but I feel I'm almost done in
and now there's nothin' left of me.

I just want my life back.
I feel that I've been hijacked.
I don't think it's too much to ask just to breathe.
I just want to breathe .

# I Want To Break Free

Quite often, life can be stifling
when we are faced with all the demands
of what is required of us from society
and the lords that rule our lands.
While I recognize that there is a system
and everything needs to be property,
sometimes I feel like a slave to it
and I really just want to break free.

# Sweet Leaf Serenade

America's first big industry was something you could smoke.
We filled fields up with tobacco so we could have a toke.
But since those days of sellin' big leafs by the pound
it's taken a different direction
cuz what goes 'round comes 'round.
Some say it's quite harmful, and think it's pretty lame
that it's killed millions of people
and we can't find someone to blame.
Yet, the smokers all say they love her
and we make accommodations.
We make special little areas
where they can share in their addictions.
But tobacco, she's an evil whore when she gets you in her grips
and if you want to live a bit longer and fuller,
I suggest you call it quits.

# [ A Breakup/Love Song for Tobacco]

Oh, I love you.

I love the way you comfort me,

the way you're always there for me,

the way you soothe me with your nicotine.

Even though you make my lungs bleed,

even though you make me smell like poverty

and make my smile look so dingy

sometimes I can't even smile at all.


I know I'm not alone.

I'm not the only one who's lost their soul

in your veil of toxic smoke.

We're all punch lines in your cruel, cruel, cruel joke.

I love you so much that I hate you

I need you, and I need you to leave me alone.

Holy smoke, I'm a dope

for ever laying my lips on you

and dragging you in to cloud up all my hope.

Oh, you got me.
I'm a slave to your evil scheme.
Just take all of my money.
I wanna feel you inside of me.

Oh, I can't breathe.
There's no doubt that you're killin' me,
but you're so good for the economy,
an all American commodity.

I know you and your good ole boys are laughin',
laughin, coughin', and jivin' your way to the bank,
and here I am, holdin' you like you're the only thing in the world
but i'm just a butt for your foolish prank.

Oh, I love you.
You've brought me moments of luxury,
but you shrouded me in your misery
so I'm lettin' you go.

It feels so good to breathe
to release that sense of urgency
to relinquish unrequited needs
and call my life my own.

So get away from me.
Leave me alone to do as I please.
Get your poisons away from me.
Goodbye, sweet tobacco.

# Free

We all want something, take it from me.
Most of us down deep just want to be free.
To be released from the shackles that bind and restrain us
and leave behind those who enslave and detain us,
to let go of attachments and ride with the wind
to not have to ask for permission again.
We all wanna be what we all wanna be
but we can never become it until we set ourselves free.

# Free Fallin'

They say freedom's just another word
for nothing left to lose.
They also say it isn't free
and gives you the power to make dreams come true.
And just because you're free
doesn't mean you're dumb,
but it does mean that you're unattached
as a general rule of thumb.
Now many who claim they have freedom
are in prisons of their own making,
finding things to attach themselves to
seems to be their greatest undertaking.
But if you really want to embrace freedom,
you've got to heed the calling,
and realize you're as free when you're flying
as you are when you are falling.

# Freedom 90

There seems to be some confusion
over what this life really offers.
Though we're told to look out for number one,
we usually fill other folks' coffers.
We're told there's life and liberty
and happiness we can pursue,
but it can be rather difficult to chase it down
when there's so much we're demanded to do.
We're told that we all have roles to fill
and tasks we must perform
because working really hard to make the rich richer
has just become the norm.
It's just the battle of the classes
and someday, we might just beat 'em.
Maybe then we'll move past servitude
and fully embrace our freedom.

# If Only

When we look upon our lives,
where we are and where we could be,
there are two big words we often bandy about,
one is IF and one is ONLY.
IF is strong enough on its own,
containing a world of possibilities.
Yet ONLY brings its limitations
and lack of acceptabilities.
We put ourselves into quite a state
with the collusion of these conjunctions.
Though we can envision the grandest of schemes,
we seem mired in life's malfunctions.
IF ONLY things were this way.
IF ONLY they were that.
IF ONLY I were someone else,
I wouldn't use this caveat.
IF ONLY she would like me.
IF ONLY he could see
the prospects that are growing deep inside of me.

IF ONLY they weren't in power.
IF ONLY things weren't the way they are,
there's no limit to what we could do,
no distance would be too far.
Yet though IF brings us a fountain of hope,
ONLY refines it to a glimmer,
and though we want to shine,
we let our glow grow dimmer.
IF ONLY should be taken out of our vocabulary
so we can realize the way life provides
is actually quite extraordinary.

If only I could play my guitar the way John Lennon did,
I would write you a better song than this.
If only I had a wall I'd paint your picture and hang it on it
and if I had a coin I'd call you, but as it is
I don't have more than what you see,
a tattered man in broken shoes
and if only that were enough for you.

Sometimes you come up short, sometimes we gotta get high.
We can't always reach the stars, but we can still reach the sky.
Sometimes you get what you want,
sometimes you take what you get,
sometimes you pray for heaven,
and sometimes you think this is it.

If only our enemies could see that we're right all the time,
they would lay their weapons down,
and there'd be no blood shed.
If only I believed all that, I could be a peaceful man.
As it is, the flag is striped in red.

Sometimes you gotta put out, sometimes you gotta give in
sometimes I'm happy to lose, sometimes I'm bitter to win
sometimes you get what you want,
sometimes you take what you get
sometimes you pray for heaven,
and sometimes you think this is it

If only no one went hungry and everyone had a place to live
and no one would ever have to help anyone else
and if only there were no need, there'd be no joy in filling it.
As it is, if there's no bad, it ain't always good.

Sometimes you run for the race, sometimes you race for the goal
sometimes you find a diamond hidden in that chunk of coal.
Sometimes you get what you want,
sometimes you take what you get
sometimes you pray for heaven,
and sometimes you think this is it

If only I could get a break, I could be a superstar
and I could have gold records on my wall and a fancy car.
As it is, all I've got are good friends, six strings,
and this beat up guitar,
and as it is, that is just enough.

# That's Life

If anyone ever told you that life is somehow fair,
they deserve a real good face smack or a kick in the derrière.
While its true that life provides and she's got plenty good at it,
fairness aint no part of it, no matter which way you spin it.
While Jefferson was poetic, he's also full of shit.
We ain't created equal, now let's get over it.
Life, it has its ups and downs, and you just gotta ride it.
Life, it may not be that fair,
but it's a hell of a lot better than dyin'.

# Wild World

We all want to find our own way
to set the course for our own path.
We each want to stand on our own two feet
to be the standout in our class.
But life can bring some challenges
whether you're a man, a woman, or child.
No matter how much you might want to tame it,
this world is certainly wild.

# You Can't Always Get What You Want

Life has a way of knowing much better
than all of the grand schemes that we've put together.
The plannin' and preppin' are all well and good
but we prob'ly do more than we probably should.
So when things don't work out the way that you thought
and the ride that you're on ain't the ticket you bought,
just try to remember as you feel your heart bleed,
life may not give what you want, but she gives what you need.

# The Bare Necessities

It's rare that I have heard animals speak
even more rare that I've heard them sing
so when they do I tend to take notice
and gather the wisdom they bring.
Even when animals are silent
I rarely see stress or concern.
They never have to worry about mortgages
or filing tax returns.
They never act like humans
and freak out over every affair.
Instead, they seem much more peaceful
as if they haven't got a care.
While humans just seem to make things worse
by catering to all their complexities,
I think the animal kingdom may just be more advanced
because they stick with the bare necessities.

# Venery

Back in the Late Middle Ages,
they came up with this concept of venery.
It started somewhere in France, in about the 14th century.
It seems that the wealthy hunters
wanted new ways to name their game,
possibly in the wild hopes that it might improve their aim.
The tradition caught on with others
and the game it started to spread
so instead of just saying "There's a group of critters!"
they called them this instead.
A group of Buffalo is an Obstinacy, and Kangaroos are Mobs
Elk form Gangs, Snakes make Nests, and Dolphins swim in Pods.
Monkeys come in a Barrels, and Pigs, they love their Passels.
Goldfish are a Troubling, but they're really not a hassle.
Woodpeckers are in a Descent,
and there's a nice Bouquet of Pheasant.
Starlings dance in Murmurations
when more than one are present.

Bullfinches like to Bellow, Peacocks have their Ostentations
Geese, they tend to Gaggle, and Eagles meet in Convocations.
There's a Conspiracy of those Lemurs
'round the Murder of the Crows,
and while Guinea Fowl are a Confusion,
try to untie a Knot of Toads.
Jaguars move in Shadows, and Lions have their Prides.
Buzzards hold a Wake, Porcupines Prickle,
and Bees, they live in Hives.
Bats are found in Cauldrons, and Cobras coil in a Quiver.
Wolves, they hunt in Packs, and Sharks, they make you Shiver.
Foxes, they Skulk, Donkeys follow Pace.
Crabs have their Consortiums.
Owls hold a Parliament, and Cockroaches are an Intrusion.
Litters are for Kittens, but Cats, they come in Clowders.
Clams are found lying in Beds,
but are much better in chowders.
Most Fish go to School, but Trout just like to Hover,
and while Nightingales tend to Watch,
Coots, they have a Cover.
Ferrets are a Business, and Baboons are a Congress.
Neither are much good at making any progress.

Apes, they come in Shrewdness upon a Sloth of Bears.

Tigers are an Ambush, and they're lurking everywhere.

Parrots are a Pandemonium

and there's a Thunder of Hippopotamuses.

Hyenas like to Cackle at the Crash of Rhinoceroses.

Armies are for Caterpillars, Herring, Frogs, and Ants.

There are many Tribes of Goats, but Parades are for Elephants.

Platypi are in a Puddle, and Gators form in Congregations.

Cheetahs have Coalitions, Wombats Wisdoms,

and Larks sing in Exaltations.

It's quite a Labor for Moles, and Giraffes, they form a Tower,

and while Grasshoppers come in a Cloud,

there's a Maelstrom of Salamanders.

Ducks fly in a Flock, but they're a Raft if they're on water,

and though Leopards like to Leap,

to get a Romp, you need some Otters.

Squirrels know how to Scurry, and Rabbits form their Warrens.

Have a Gulp of Cormorants, a Kettle of Hawks,

or try a Siege of Herons.

It's a Pitying for Turtle Doves, and Gorillas form a Band.

There's a Kaleidoscope of Butterflies,

and Flamingos like to Stand.

There's a Flock of Sheep, a Jellyfish Bloom,
and Martens have their Richness.
While Ravens are known for Unkindness,
who wouldn't love a Charm of Finches?
Penguins live in Colonies, and Quails are in their Coveys.
Jays throw Parties, Weasels Sneak,
and Swans, they have their Bevies.
Snails have Hoods, Lobsters are a Risk, and Zebras do have Zeal.
Just think that all these names started out
as just other words for meals.
That's what I know about venery, and I hope you like what I did
because I'll never get a round of applause
from an Audience of Squid.

# I Don't Need Anything

In a world that tells me all that I need
that makes my wallet hemorrhage and my bank account bleed,
I'm told every day I need this and that
to fill my every desire without getting fat,
but beyond all the bluster and veiled innuendo,
I know there's some dude seein' just what he can do
to take some of my stuff so that his pile gets bigger,
and it's all done with plenty of vim and with vigor.
Cuz the economy has gotta grow to reach maximum size.
There's gotta be somebody who just has to claim the prize.
But as he's blowin' his horn and I can finally see past,
I know I don't need anything, I don't need anything I don't have.

# The People That Make You

Whatever we're goin through and wherever we're goin',
there's a number of people that we end up knowin'
that help us become the people we are
by teaching us lessons about the world near and far.
They talk us through problems and help us through issues
and when we really need it, they offer us tissues.
Sometimes they're friendly and sometimes they're mean,
sometimes they're lovers and sometimes enemies,
but each and every one, whether they cheer or berate you,
the people around you are the people that make you.

# The People That Made Me

I'd like to introduce you to some people of notice.
I want you to know how they affect now.
All the lost souls and cherry bowls
that have dappled my moments
as I've sought how to live right and they've shown me how.
Each of the people that have loved me and left me
have done so for the better and I hope that they're healthier
for getting to know me and walking beside me,
my lovers and brothers that have grown up in life with me.
I am so grateful
that these are the people that made me.


My nuclear family gave great radiation,
and each family since has brought great celebration.
As I've wandered through the lives and loves
of schemers and dreamers,
I've imprinted desires and learned lessons that reverb
a rate that has guided my direction and decision,
they have crafted my mission and focused my vision.

They have all helped to make me the man that I may be.
Like 'em or lump 'em,
these are the people that made me.

I am what I am from the journey that I have been on,
from the ones that have shared in my steps
and shared in my song.
We create one another like a mirror creates a reflection.
Can you see yourself when you give it some closer inspection?

I've got digital connections through ones and through zeros
to all kinds of whack jobs and all kinds of heroes,
world changers, game players, critics and lackeys,
head nodders, back stabbers, cheerleaders and wannabes.
We're all connected now as we filter excuses,
run up our white flags and establish our truces.
We trust one another just more than Big Brother
but we know if we do this, we gotta do it together.
These are my people.
These are the people that make me.

This is the new world, the new revolution,
where we all discover if we can guide evolution,
and make the world better by making connections,
and forgiving our faults to see the beauty beyond them.
Each of us flawed and each of us sinners,
each of us champions and each of us winners.
Open your eyes to the people around you,
to make the world better we can't do it without you,
so love as you're able
because these are the people that make you.

# Danny Boy

All of us have a Danny Boy,
someone we love in our life,
someone who must follow their own path
yet their leaving cuts like a knife.
We hate to see them go
but we know that they must leave us,
and their parting brings us sorrow
and leaves us feeling grievous.
But we love them just the same,
and we wish them all the best,
and we do our best not to let them see
the pain that's in our chest.
For those we love, we let them go
to make their life an art,
and though they may be gone, they're a part of us
for they live within our heart.

# Castle on a Hill

Some of us have positive memories
of the childhoods we led,
and we remember fondly
as we look at the road ahead
the people who helped us on our path
and contributed to our being
by encouraging us in all of our goals
and helping us with our seeing
visions of what we can be
and all the places we could go,
but whatever horizons we may run toward
there's nothing quite like coming home.

# Be Here Now

With all the roaming I've always done,
setting in a new place for every sun,
I've seen the world and the beauty within it,
and I can't help but to be in love with it.
Not a day goes by I don't find myself grateful
amidst all of the angry and all of the hateful.
If you wanna be happy, let me tell you how.
Let go of the bullshit and just be here now.

# Every Little Thing

Making a difference in the world
doesn't need to be a big, grand gesture.
We don't really need any great big schemes.
What we need is something lesser.
While it's great that people have vision
and are developing all sorts of plans,
all that stuff is worthless
without willing hearts and hands.
Great feats are accomplished
by little tasks done well,
and when we enjoy the little parts we play,
that's how we excel.
Because life happens in the moment
not in the outcomes to which we cling
so give your best in all that you say and do
and be grateful for every little thing.

These are troubled times we're going through
and every one of us has so much to do
it can be so hard to know just where to start.
So feel your breath for the gift it is
giving you life so you can live.
Every little thing starts with the beat of your own heart.

The human race is off and running.
Some of us are kind and some of us are cunning,
and some of us just don't know where we belong.
But if you see a need that you can fulfill,
there's joy in the service and joy in the skill,
and every little thing you do makes us all strong.

Everywhere you look, trouble abounds
in every little city and every little town,
and every little thing seems bigger than it really is.
Every little thing adds to every little thing
and every little thing gives us something else to cling
to as we try to figure out every little thing that's hers and his.

Every little person's trying to figure out
every little question and every little doubt
and every little thing that we don't understand.
We all feel alone in this great big world,
and it don't matter if you're a boy or a girl,
spread a little love to every woman and every man.

Every little thing that you say and do,
every why, how, and when, it comes back to who.
Be somebody who makes the world a better place.
Offer up a smile or a helping hand.
Spread a little love to every woman and man.
Every little thing's a little step in the human race.

Every little thing's complexer than it needs to be.
You and me and he and she make we.
This big old Earth is one big family tree,
and every little thing you give makes us all more free.

So as simple as you feel that it may be
to withdraw from the world
cuz they're all crazy
and sit back and do nothing
as every little thing goes wrong,
to fully live your life,
you must participate
and if you do it with a smile
that'd really be great,
and we'll keep
making every little thing right up
as we move along.

# THE JOURNEY AHEAD

To find the freedom we're looking for and release ourselves from the prisons we've created, we need to take Regina Spektor's advice when she says that "You've Got Time" and that's most of what we need as we play "The Game" of life. As the cowboy continues down his path, he's got to connect with SOJA and say "I Believe" that no matter what you do, it all comes back to you so that when we see the challenges life offers us, we'll at least say "I'll Try".

But trying isn't always enough. You've got to "Follow Through" as Gavin Degraw says. To overcome the challenges on the path ahead, we've got to accept Matisyahu's challenge to "Live Like A Warrior" and sing Rachel Platen's "Fight Song". It also wouldn't hurt to take some of that rebellion from the Eighties and "Cum On Feel The Noise" with Quiet Riot to let the powers that be know that like Twisted Sister, "We're Not Gonna Take It".

If we can cowboy up, we can answer David Bowie's call to be "Heroes" and realize along with Queen that "We Are The Champions".

# You've Got Time

Time is a prison for all of us and we all gotta pay our dues
and when it really drags on, we can't help but sing the blues.
But if we see it for what it really is and all the gifts it brings,
time can be our bestest friend, the reason our heart sings.
If we take all our moments and get to fill them up
with what we love and who we love, and it don't get corrupt,
we got ourselves a pretty good life, but it ain't always so,
especially when so much of our time is off to work we go.
So when you've got those extra moments,
when the workin' day is done,
and you've satisfied the masters of das capital is um,
be sure to fill those moments with rhythm and with rhyme
cuz when it all comes down to it, all we've got is time.

# The Game

What we got right here in this game called life
is a labyrinth of ups and downs, victories and strife.
You try to play by the rules but they're always changin',
try to follow the pattern as its rearrangin',
and it seems like somebody's always pulling the strings,
makin things happen and makin things change,
but when you get back to playin things right,
when you release the controls and give up the fight,
stop trying to force things and stop trying to blame,
you'll find life provides if you just play the game.

Everything I need is right here with me.
All the living I can do I'll do right now.
All I ask of life is she provide for me,
keep me safe, not always warm, loved, not always held,
just keep me fed and keep me in the game.
I see beauty in the storm as she engulfs me
as I'm dashed against the rocks amid the waves.
Though the storm she beats, she batters, and she bruises,
she enchants and charms and seems to know the way.
Though some say I follow blindly, I'm an apprentice,
and I follow my guide 'round each and every turn.
Though the lessons are before me,
between my blinks, behind my breath,
only when I see them will I learn.
Though I may never understand all the answers,
all the whispers in the shadows, in the brush,
and I cry out to my God, "Please tell me of eternity,"
He just shrugs and smiles and asks me, "What's the rush?"
And if I don't stop waiting on yesterday,
and tomorrow looks more bleak than today,
I may open my eyes, but I'll never see,
it plays me if I don't play the game.

# I Believe - Part 2

We got this thing called karma,

and some say it's all in the mind,

this idea of universal justice

that really isn't all blind.

Matter of fact, some aren't too cool with karma,

and they call her a bitch,

but it's a real good thing she does what she does

and has gone and found her niche.

Cuz she's only bad when you're screwing around,

not doing things that you should,

and when she whispers what you're supposed to do

it'd be better if you would.

But when you got yourself some virtue

and use purpose in your actions,

karma tends to lift you up

and offer you some traction.

It's a simple little formula,

the magic she unfolds,

you get out of life what you give it

so you might as well give it your all.

# I'll Try

I spent some time there underneath the Bodhi tree,
not long enough, I'm not a patient man.
Dharma don't come easy for a guy like me.
I hope I think I wonder if I can.
Each day I keep on workin' in my wicked ways.
It seems the only thing that's killing me is me,
a wanderer who's givin' up his rambling ways,
an outlaw who can't pay the penalty,
but I'll try, oh, I will try.

This world has got no use now for a dreamer.
If I don't punch in then I don't get my pay.
I need to be a mover and a schemer,
but this poet's mind just doesn't work that way.
Your brave new world is really startin' to scare me.
Where I fit in I haven't got a clue.
I would rise to every challenge when you dare me,
but you've given me just oh so much to do.
but I'll try, oh, I will try

My mind tends to wander and my body follows.
A single thought is never on my mind.
Every day is yesterday as well as tomorrow,
thoughts are racin' to keep up with time.
If only I could make you see what I'm goin' through.
If only I could make you understand.
This heart on my sleeve is all I have to offer you.
My mind just cannot conceive your plan,
but I'll try, oh, I will try
I will try
to find my way.

# Follow Through

Every time we make one of those decisions
that puts us on mission and gives us new direction,
we're faced with a whole new set of dilemmas
'bout how to better ourselves to make the world better.
The road to hell may be laid with our best intentions
but it also goes the other way, directly toward heaven.
It's all in perspective, the way that you see it,
but when you say you'll do something,
we all hope that you mean it.
Though we all sometimes bite off more than we can chew,
tryin' ain't nearly as satisfying as some good follow through.

# Live Like a Warrior

Our society tends to like warfare and blowing things to pieces.
We promise ourselves that there'll be peace
once the bombing ceases.
Though I think there's better ways of getting through our strife,
there's still a certain nobility
in the person that lays down their life
for something bigger than his own concerns
or what she thinks she wants,
those who throw themselves into action
when they see the need for response.
In the heat of battle, you lose yourself
and become one with the moment.
There's no need for forgiveness
and no need to ask for atonement.
So if you're fighting with yourself,
and your past has become a barrier,
I advise you to just let it go,
and start living like a warrior.

# Fight Song

We often underestimate our own capabilities
and magnify meekness through all our gentilities,
but it's good to remember what we have within
and finding the place where we can begin
to let the fire within us grow into a blaze
and let others around us be shocked and amazed
when we no longer allow ourselves to be put down,
when we plant our flag and hold our ground
because we know what we're worth and our right to belong
and we let the world know when we sing our fight song.

# Cum On Feel the Noise

I tended to love the Eighties
and the way that the music was played.
I really dug them electric guitars
and the distorted sounds that they made.
It was a fabulous time for rebellion
against what we didn't really care.
The greatest real concern we had
was how we groomed our hair.
But it got us up and got us out,
they called it the me generation.
Some say it was the decline
of western civilization.
The Eighties were the decade
that most men became boys.
All that was asked if you played along
was that you cum on feel the noise.

# We're Not Gonna Take It

When we started the American experiment,
we wanted democracy,
and we did the best we could
with an aristocracy.
But what we're dealing with now
is an animal of a different breed.
There are a few who wish to fulfill their every desire
while many are struggling with needs.
We sacrifice all of our time and well being
so we can increase a few people's wealth.
We'll burn up all the Earth has to offer
and gamble with our health.
Some have been trained this is the way things should be,
there needs to be rich and poor,
but quite a few still want equality
and we're not gonna take anymore.

# Heroes

There's a call that goes out to heroes
to be of help to others.
They come in the form of strangers,
teachers, friends, and mothers.
We don't need an invitation
and we don't need an appointment.
We can be heroes for a day
or we can be heroes for a moment.
We can't be heroes all the time
because there just isn't the need.
Sometimes we need to follow.
Sometimes we need to lead.
So when you feel that call
asking you to be of service,
know that all of this is designed
so that you can meet your purpose.

# We Are The Champions

In every battle we have,
there are winners and there are losers,
and in the battle of life,
there are givers and there are users.
But the real battle that we're fighting
is for our dignity,
and laying claim to that victory
is our responsibility.
If we believe in ourselves,
we can change how this story ends.
If we can stand up for each other,
then we are the champions, my friends.

# *Epilogue*

After all is said and done, I'm glad I took time to write.

I hope I made ya stop and think,

and maybe offered a bit of insight.

What I'd really like to leave you with

as you head out on your way

is one more little nugget of hope to help you make it day to day.

The world is bigger than you think it is,

bigger than all of your troubles,

so take a deep breath right here and right now

and turn all of your worries to bubbles.

Let 'em drift up and out through the roof,

and later when you go outside,

you'll see all those distant worries as stars up in the sky.

And as you head on down your trail

and see others tryin' to find their way,

at least give them a smile as well,

and tell 'em ole Cowboy said "Hey".

Cuz we're all on our own adventure,
and we're all on our own little quest.
Some are trying to makes themselves better,
and some are striving to be the best.
Some have taken bad tumbles, been kicked in the head,
and got lost in the woods more than once,
and if you take their nonsense too personally,
you really are some kinda dunce.
We all ain't let go of our worries,
and some have forgotten how to laugh or to smile,
and if you can't learn to forgive and let go,
a better world might take awhile.

But if you look past the horizon
and see a future bright and clear,
I hope you cowboy up,
and I hope it starts right here.

www.ingramcontent.com/pod-product-compliance
Lightning Source LLC
Chambersburg PA
CBHW051727040426

42447CB00008B/1006